Staying Soft

Poems to restore your heart to softness in Christ.

By the Holy Spirit and Maranatha

With 11 Igbo Poems and their English translations

Staying Soft

Biblical references and quotations from KJV (King James' Version).

ISBN: 979-8-9871742-3-4

Edited by Olatunde Obafemi

Illustrations by Maranatha
Igbo translations by Nnaemeka Felix Nnaemeka (Snr)

First printing edition 2024.
Onefirm Media Corp.
PO Box 186
New York, NY 10031

▸ Dedication ◂

To my Abba, Yeshua & Helper; I love You now and in eternity. You are perfect in all Your ways. My Yahweh, *Aha gi di uto n'onu m*[1]. I give to You this book that You have given the world through me.

To my dad, through whom Abba sent me this gift of writing and a way with words. Thank you for the Igbo translations for some of my poems. The time I spent sitting with you to write each one, surrounded by your praises and mocking laughter at my inability to spell some Igbo words, I will never forget those moments.

To Amanda, Damini my damsel, who believed in me even when I could not find the heart to do so. Thank you for putting your heart into anything I say 'yes' to. Where would I be without your compassion and commitment?

And to Fems, my answered prayer. Thank you for taking this book, Softie, as your own and co-parenting with me. I love you and so does Softie.

1 Igbo sentence transliterated as 'Your Name is sweet in my mouth'.

▸ Prayer ◂

Genesis 1:31 - And God saw every thing that he had made, and, behold, it was very good.

I pray that you begin to see yourself as good, that good thing that God made and became pleased with Himself.

I pray that you gain the ability to express the fullness of your humanity and identity through the talents He has given you, for the purpose Abba has called you to, and that it flourishes a little more every moment you live.

I pray that you learn to come to Abba with all you are, whether good or bad, and that your fellowship with Him never breaks. I pray that you are able to bring every aspect of your life to Jesus, no compartmentalization, and let Him see you naked—as you are, without shame.

And I pray that you really LIVE the life that Abba has designed for you by remaining in unbroken, intimate fellowship with Him.

—

'THIS IS A KIND OF KNOWLEDGE THAT COMES WITH FERVOUR. THE ZEAL OF THE LORD WILL DO IT.'

Table of Content

► An Important Introduction ◄

The poems in this collection tell many seemingly disjointed but united stories. They are united by the fact that one person, me, has experienced them. So, they tell of a world from my point of view.

This is a story that I am telling, but it is about me and about you, too. As you read through—do it slowly. These poems will spark within you an expression that you may have struggled to understand, or simply give you the words for a feeling you have always had.

Since a majority of our existence is clothed in words, the ones we utter and the ones we hold, we fulfil an unspoken obligation by finding the right ones.

I have always kept the dates of everything I have written to be able to trace what phase of my life inspired that piece. I have included these dates and some who know me might be able to pinpoint where I have been; from first meeting Christ to going deeper in Him. For others, it might only create a trail from where I used to be to where I am now. Whatever the case, I hope it is something you enjoy doing. To make it a bit of a puzzle, I have not arranged these pieces chronologically.

Many of these poems have the same dates. This is because I

had written verses sparingly before but in the time (December 2023) during which I realised God's Hand was in this, His zeal also came upon me and I started to write poems every single day; many of them during prayers and conversations with God. In two weeks I had written over 50 poems, some of which did not make it here for the sake of the seniors[2].

My aim, which I know will be achieved, is to take you through so many emotions to keep you tuned to and overwhelmed at the wealth of expression at the same time.

In my over twenty years of living, I have seen over and again that many of us humans want to know that we are not alone in the things that we feel, and the emotions that we cannot express for the fear that we would be the only ones. I want you to feel human, not in the commonly powerless sense but with a deepened awareness of your humanity in the way God designed you to be and feel.

You might have a spirit that communes with God but dear one, God made you very human, too. He wants you to enjoy good food, have healthy friendships, feel deeply, be in touch with your emotions (re-examining them through His eyes) and enjoy human life in its fullness. Christ has changed humanity from its post-Adamic roughness to holy softness.

2 Older poems of the author written before December 2023.

We can learn to *stay soft* despite our many hard experiences in this world. **The only way to unlock this softness and beauty in this fallen earth is through UNBROKEN fellowship with and obedience to Yahweh.**

You are not alone. And as you read my mind on things that often harden people like unforgiveness, heartbreak, situation-ships, death, fatigue, vis-a-vis the solution to all of them, Christ - who has become such a deep part of my life that He is woven into every verse if you look deeply (or not) - I know you will realise this. You will also find better, healthier ways to think about these emotions in a way that softens your heart. Maybe laugh at some of the others. **Mostly, you will give thanks—gratitude to God has a way of softening our hearts.**

We do not just need Jesus for our eternity: we need Him to make peace with our past, enjoy our present and have a future to look forward to. No matter how bad, everything is made *good* when we bring it to Jesus. EVERYTHING. Only a life enjoyed through Christ looks forward to heaven; even more, to the coming of Jesus.

I might not have experienced all you have and some of my experiences here might not tally with yours, but JESUS is what we have in common. He saved both you and me, He holds peace in His hands as water to quench our parched throats.

I do not believe that what is secular must be anti-Christ, this is untrue. In some of these poems I might not be preaching to you, but everything I impart is laced with truth and will have you thinking deeply too, about life and these topics I touch. Many of these have become prayers for me, *'lift up my eyes to meet Your gaze, lighten my heart to contain You.'*

However, there's nothing I would say in these pages, that your heart does not already know. I only ask, permit me to remind you.

1

Slow eating

I think food should be eaten
slowly.
And drinks should be sipped
silently.
A gorged mouth finds no *taste to remember.*

In this carrot stew, I tasted novelty.
In this *ofe-akwu*[3], I tasted home.
In this rice, I tasted strength.
In this *lasagna,* I tasted exoticness.
And with my tongue, I have stepped in places
I have never been with my feet.

When we eat
and our body does its thing;
what lingers?
Is it not the taste

3 A popular Nigerian soup and delicacy from the Igbo Tribe and the Niger Delta made from palm nuts.

retrieved by the tongue?

So, let us eat slowly;
that when our stomachs are filled,
we hear quickly
and desist from gluttony.

My tongue *remembers the taste*
of what it held a little longer;
what my teeth ground a little while,
as my mind looked in my mouth
pondering on an explosion of flavour.
Not distracted by a screen;
for *food should be eaten in isolation.*

This is the kind of nourishment
that enriches not just the body, but the soul.
— 09/Feb/24.

2

Cheap Chocolate

Today I am *tired*:
The taste of cheap chocolate on my tongue
Memories of friends' laughter starting to fade
Bones aching from long and short strides
Oil gathering at the tip of my nose

Today I am *numb*:
Staring into space
Hoping something can come from nothing
Writing words that mean nothing to me
Telling myself that I'll be ok

Today I am *speechless*:
I form the words but they don't come out
My ears tickle as my eyes water
I stare at the ceiling to keep the tears from heeding gravity

Today I am *dead*:
My body won't move, it can't.
I watch my fingers turn cold

Maranatha

The words in my mouth become sand;
I close my eyes.

There is a void in my soul:
I am in a dark pit
Then I see a Hand reach down to pull me up
Who is *this* Man?

My hesitation does not faze Him
and after the longest time
I reach out of my darkness
to take His hand.
He grips me and in His touch *I feel love.*

When I wake up
I am new.
And there is Life within me
that lights up my view.
— 14/Apr/22.

3

Overwhelming goodness

I am overwhelmed by His Goodness;
for Abba has given me ease and speed.
My heart remains at peace
while my feet race ahead.

The Lord has made my life profitable to Him
For every talent I have returned another:
The ROI[4] is high,
He blots out my mistakes.

I thought the world was shaking me
but it was my Lord shaking the world
to adjust to me.

My Deliverer,
You have opened my eyes:
I see beyond me
Now I see my family

4 Return On Investment.

Maranatha

I see my church
I see my friends
and I see You in all of them.

You saved, raised me, kept me.
You matured me, taught me to worship:
to enjoy Your Presence, sitting with You
To move when You move.

So many hard choices
but the easiest has always been *choosing* You.

You have made me a priest in my house:
You have sharpened my ears to hear
and my eyes to see;
while my hands do.

My mouth is full of wise counsel:
a strange fire flames within me;
a flame that burns those who come close
but they are not consumed, only *refined.*
— 23/Dec/23.

4

4C hair!

Self-love is:
washing my natural hair, myself
even though it breaks my back.
Not adding sugar to my tea.
Telling my secrets to someone I trust;
because a shared burden is easier carried.

Self-love is:
keeping quiet when my words become daggers on my tongue;
to keep from hurting my neighbour.
Putting on lip balm instead of biting my lips.
Wearing clothes I do not have to hold down.

Self-love is:
waking up at 4 am to pray because I said I would.
Knowing what parts of myself to give out and the parts to selfishly guard.
Genuinely celebrating my friend who's received something I've wanted all year.

Self-love is being me, in every way I can be.
Not fitting into anyone else's mould but Christ's.
And self-love is writing these words and hoping you feel it too.
And that it changes some part of you…
for good.
— 13/Apr/22.

5

Pondering

I stay pondering on my Lord
when sleep refuses to take me.
I pour my heart out to Jesus;
my being is engulfed by Him.

What a delight
to be owned, made and known
by You, O Most High!
Day in and out, I see Your Goodness.

Remember me, Lord.

I am not forgotten.

Adonai, El-Shaddai
El-Roi, I am always in Your Sight.

How You move among Your people;
a wonder!
How You deliver us from shackles;
a plunder…

My heart beats for You.
My being moves for You.
You have filled my ears with signs
and my mouth with Your Testimony.

What a mighty God!
The Lion and the Lamb.
Multi-faceted, beyond comprehension…
Who is like You?
Who can be like You?
— 21/Dec/23.

6

When I die

When I die,
I want to leave bits and p i e c e s of me everywhere.
Large and small.
In the words I've written
and the pictures I've taken.
In the people I've given a dose of my laughter
and the ones that have taken up my time
while I lived.

When I die,
I want a bit of my soul to lin
ger
in the words I liked to say
and the people I loved to love.
In the spaces I have thrived
and the places I have been
while I lived...

When I die,
I want to be that forgotten dream

triggered by the littlest of things;
before it fades away—giving you no chance to grab it wholly.
I want to be at the corner, unnoticeable;
unless you reach for me.

And no more tears,
I want to make you smile when you think
of all the things I did...
while I lived.
— 17/Apr/22.

7

Dawn

Early in the morning
as my lids are released from the cage of sleep—
My lips will greet You.
My heart will exalt You.
And my spirit will worship You.

My soul will wait for Your Instructions
concerning all that lay before me in the day.
O Holy Spirit! What are we doing today?
I will not move if You don't.
I receive healing from the traumas of yesterday.

How can I move without You?
I am nothing without Your many Graces.
Each day,
my soul is stretched weary without Your
yesses and nos that guide me through the day.
Each day,
my heart feels empty when I haven't—
Spoken to my Lover,

called on His Name,
written Him a song…

I become devoid of good wisdom.
A liability to all around me.

Yes, one who hasn't heard
from God for the day
is a liability to those around Him.
— 26/Dec/23.

8

Unrest

There is unrest within me;
My soul is not quiet.
I came before my Lord, this morning,
and my heart did not sing.
My lips did not move.
My hands did not clap.

'But don't you remember,
all the miracles of yesterday?
How He led you to victory
despite the odds?'
I asked my soul
'Why rebel against your Lord?'

It wouldn't budge.
Still I stayed.
Helpless...
until my helplessness cried out
Jesus, help me!
Jesus, help me I cannot see You!

Open my eyes, let me see You!

My Lord came, quickly.
'*Be of good cheer,*' He said.
'*I have overcome the world.*'
Then my heart started to beat again.
The numbness dissolving into tears;
I remembered, I remember...

Now my Lord has freed me
from the stronghold of forgetfulness.
How could I move without my Lord?
A day without creates a void in me
that is quickly filled by *anti-life.*
What is fish outside water?
A dead fish.

The sweetest of men is my Lord.
The most handsome of men is He.
Grace has flown from His lips
to revive my soul.
I will stay with You forever.
— 21/Dec/23.

Confirmation

Confirmations upon confirmations.
Opportunities upon opportunities.
My Lord's Hand is wide open to bless me.
No, I don't believe in coincidences.

And this is how I know the Lord is here:
the doors are swinging open;
my name is uttered in places I'm not.

In my hand is nestled obedience.
I will serve with all my heart.
I will serve in my Father's house.
I will serve the body of Christ.

And goodness is rising within me.
In speaking in the spirit
I hear the wonders of Him.
Wonderful things happening in the spirit
to manifest in the physical and bring joy.

And who will a Father speak to
if not His children?
The Lord is speaking.

Let us listen.

The Lord is moving.

Let us move.

Let our Abba tell us secret things
as children with the mind of Christ.
For family matters cannot be discussed with strangers;
in stillness we will hear.

Our confidence is
that Your Thoughts are higher;
that Your Ways are higher.
And You always act
on behalf of Your Word, Promises:
Your Love and Loyalty to us.

When our minds are distracted
Yours never is, can never be.
You bring to mind what is important,
setting our eyes on things above.
Through Your Apostles, Prophets and Teachers
revival is coming!

Be strong and courageous.
These signs will follow
them that believe.
And revival is coming…
— 03/Jan/24.

10

Greet your mother

When you feel tired, have breakfast.
When you feel tired, get up and use the bathroom.
When you feel tired, smile and greet your mother.

Fatigue is an unconscious mix of *fear* and *numb.*
To fight it is to disparage its hold on you
by doing the familiar, though banal:
strengthen your will and trick your body to do the things it has always done.
Then it will not work against you.

And when you can do the banal
until it flows into your spirit,
becoming one with your will—
You become the magician that tricks the crowd to see a rabbit where there's none.
You become the musician who sings tunes that ignite emotions in a dead soul.
You become the healer giving medicine to wake a sleeping heart.

Then you can do the impossible and never-before-done.

Then you will rise above fear, doubt,
and do what is required of you.
For to stop moving is to be left behind in the procession of life.
What happens to a seed *who* refuses the nutrients of the earth?
Even death would be a mercy.

The days of tiredness, when your body works against your will
are your chance to prove
that you do all you do
for a reason beyond you.
You're simply a stream in a vast ocean.
A beat in the ever-pulsating heart of life.
Why should life go on without you
when it can go on with you?
You're a beauty that life can do without.
But why should it?
To whose profit would that be?

Every day is a new song that life sings
and we must make our hands and legs, our hearts
learn this strange rhythm we have never heard.
So we can start the dance and revel in its twists and turns.
And sometimes we like the song too much, we don't want to stop singing;

even though we must forget the tune and sing another tomorrow.
And other times, the song of the day is agony to our ears;
we stop listening before it stops playing;
willing to listen to tomorrow's song before it plays.

But we forget, that life's songs are but one song, split into many tunes;
with the power given to compose and change the notes.
We can let it sing to us and be content with listening.
Or we can say 'no' and alter the notes for another song to play.
Power lies in the hands of those who will take it.

Find hidden strength in your fingers.
Lock eyes with strangers whose spirits you have dined with at the Master's table.
Think about your breath, whom you ignore
while giving credit to your eyes when they flutter open.
Their fragile strength holds your life.

And when it goes dark,
remember that *Who sent you*
is right *behind you.*
Let Him be your means—
And your end.
— 20/Oct/22.

11

Rain dance

Situationships are like
dancing in the rain.
You know you should not be doing it
but it's okay as long as you're not alone.

But then you look around and realise
your partner's gone.
He waves from a window and thick sweater.
And now you're shivering in the cold, alone.

And you'll hope that the next time
that someone calls you out to play in the rain—
They have an umbrella.
— 01/May/22.

12

Protect

He protects my rest.
He keeps my feet from
the path of mistakes.

If I venture there
He brings me back.
If I tread there
He sends His Word;
through a friend, a mentor or a stranger
to bring me back to His will.

When my judgement was clouded
and my hands longed for action;
He sent a friend to warn me.
He made my mouth open
to provoke the wise counsel of a good friend.

My heart sickens when I think
of the imminent unrest You saved me from.
I am terrified that I would ruin me;

struggling when He gave me ease.

Yet again, I am made aware
of how foolish and lost I am
without God.

Where would I be?

If God did not go before me?
Foreseeing my obstacles and overcoming them?

Many are the plans in a man's heart
but blessed is the man
who allows God to advise him
and His plans to take centre-stage.

When I forget
He sends a reminder.
He is on my side.
He won't let His Investment go bad.
So, He saves me from *me*.

Jesus, I was sure
that I was on the right path.
But even in the wrong place
my eyes encountered possibilities.
My heart forgave.
My hands were willing to work.
Even here, I have received Instruction.
I have learnt a lesson.

Now, with a coincidence, a conversation
I see a clearer picture.
The time was not yet.
My heart knows this to be true.
He reveals the error I made
in my thinking.
Clouded with emotions
but a pure heart still.

Now, I see that my desire
aligns with my Lord's.
Why else would He bring
this to my notice?
Not because my choice was wrong
but He didn't want mixture or combination.
Only focus, on the thing He'd
handpicked for me, and led me to.

He has given me rest.
No way I am getting out of it.

And even if I did not listen
to wise counsel
and made the terrible mistake;
my Abba is big enough
to amend my ways
and restore.
My Abba is big enough

to turn evil to good.

Life may be heavy
but His Word carries light;
and they have a resting place in my heart.
— 09/Jan/24.

13

Hunter

Strengthen his heart as he searches for me;
do not let him become weary.
Keep his eyes on You;
so when he finds me, he knows what to do.

Keep the smile on his face
and the vigour in his pace.
Keep the certainty in his heart,
until they cross—our paths.

Fill him with Your goodness.
His life with Your fullness.
Let His dreams come true.
As long as they're in sync with You.

Make him happy as he is.
He knows You, let his joy be found in this.
And when he finds me, let that joy double.
Let it be an end to many troubles.

Fill him with Your wisdom.
Let him bring glory to Your Kingdom.
Guide him on the path to take.
The path of righteousness, for Your Namesake.

Let those who dig a pit for him fall in it.
When they make evil plans for him, let them take the hit.
For in You he moves and has his being.
He lays on Your altar, a sacrifice that is living.

And when he finds me, let him know.
And when I am found, let me know.
There lies no emptiness within us;
But together, we'll become much more.

We were never incomplete;
but together, we'll become whole.
— 31/Dec/23.

14

Megharia

Dele duu machoputa ebe ime joro ihe
Ka-iwe megharia ha
Mgbe ime joro ihe, dele duu
Ka ihapu ime ka iwe dakwa si gi

N'ime i dele duu
Enwere nkuputa, imezi-ihe na ndozi.

Amend

Be quiet and notice your error.
So that you can make amends.
When in the wrong, cease speaking.
Incur no more wrath.

In silence,
there is confession, correction
and reconciliation.
— 31/Dec/23.

15

Fear of the Lord

The fear of the Lord
has seized my heart.
He may do as He pleases
but with my good in mind.
I do not always understand
but I do not need to.

He watches me from heavens
commanding the elements to favour me
and angels to flank me.

When He decides a thing
who can stop Him?
My Abba is only limited by His Words
by His Faithfulness, Promises to me.
Like the rainbow of Noah
that encircles His throne.

Who is like the Almighty?
He declares a thing and it happens.

Every life is submitted to Him.
Nothing can stand against Him.

He does what He has in mind.
He has so many things in mind for me.
One who is more invested in my life
than I could ever be.
What a God!

He knows what He is doing
and only for the clean in heart;
only for those who will trust Him beyond understanding,
will there be blessings beyond understanding.

I am committed to this God.
I have seen many alternatives
but none like or above Him
for this One is too mindful of me.

He shushes me before I speak evil.
He embraces me from within
when no man can comfort me.
He warns me in dreams,
opening my eyes in visions.
He strengthens my hands to work
and my heart to serve.
He hides me in light,
the darkness cannot perceive me.

He awakens my zeal in different paths,
telling me it is all possible when He is with me.
He protects my interests.

He has taught me by Himself.
I know Him in my heart.
I know His voice.
He is my shepherd, I have all I need.
And if I don't have it, I don't need it.
For the Almighty is my gold
and my finest silver.
— 10/Jan/24.

16

The lid

The lid slips
and out he peeps.

'Finally I can get in
without being seen.

'Ouch!' the pain spreads
from his fingers to his head.

Pain explodes
I secure my abode

My face has a weary smile
and for the fourth time this week,
I whisper
'Not today Despair.'
— 10/Nov/22.

17

Joy

I've never felt this happy,
this joyful, this soft.
God is my Father,
He never falters in His responsibility.

He takes such good care of me
I cannot complain.
And this is not just for good,
even in adversity, *He is my portion.*
He is my satisfaction.
My gold and my finest silver.

He favours me, everyday:
Men help me with smiling faces.
When I voice my desire
He commands the world to help.
Sending angels to my aid.

I am satisfied:
My heart is full.

The Lord has blessed me
with a gift that blessed me
and blesses others, too.

It gets better everyday, until
I leave this world;
because I am going deeper in Him.

The Lord brought me before the wise,
giving me access to wisdom
from my elders;
it is not what I could buy.

Worry has no place in me.
It meets peace at my gates
and turns back.
What He wills, only that will be.

When I set goals
He holds my hand to accomplish them.
He makes a way for me.
All I have to do, is pay each day its due.
And for that, there is strength, too.

I serve You with all my strength.
At home, church.
This is the key to my fulfilment.
You have done me well.
— 12/Feb/24.

18

Overwhelmed

Why do I only write
when love overwhelms me
or when I feel none of it?

Why do I remember my pen when you whisper the sweetest words?
Or when you leave, not even a trace of your shadow?

I want that place, that grey area.
I want to write about loving you when I cannot see or hold you.
I want to write about dead butterflies.
I want to write about knowing just enough to hold on.

I want to write about a loose grip that works
            because holding on too tight hurts.
I want to write about the silence
            and miles of space.

I want to write about hope too.

Hope that hurts but doesn't burn.
Hope that tethers me to you.
Hope, that might be my undoing
when all is said and done; and you are not mine.
— 13/Apr/22.

19

Back to worship

I bring my mind back to the place of worship
from its thousand thoughts and wanderings
to focus on the beauty of my Lord.
What is worship if my mind is absent?

Love the Lord with your heart, mind, strength[5].
All of it, all of each.
Let your spirit connect to His.
Let not your mind wander.
Instead, let it wonder
and with your vigour, sing praises.
Clap your hands and dance.

Let all of me
come before You.
Let those who praise Him
praise Him with understanding.
— 26/Dec/23.

5 Mark 12:30 or Matthew 22:37.

20

Mene mene tekel

מנא מנא תקל ופרסין

I used to be free
even more than the law would decree.
Do it when I want it,
no need for deceit.

In trance I reached out,
the fruit in Eve's mouth.
Mene mene tekel[6],
freedom lost, not by a shekel.

Trapped by iron bars.
All I thought I gained, a farce.
Sneaky sneaky, now on tiptoe.
Never to let anyone know.

More hope than I, the proud king had.
For my case was purely labelled bad.

---

6 Daniel 5:25-28.

But mindful He is, the One above,
Who deemed me worthy, and topped it with love.
— Feb/2016.

21

Rest

Toiling
An embraced curse.
A pain that becomes a succour
that we cannot do without.

No one holds on to their demons
tighter than one who forgets what home looks like.

The One who has placed this work in your hands,
this blessing and curse;
what will He say to this now?

Do what you can and do it well.
Rest when you can and rest well.
For what is urgent today, may be
forgotten tomorrow;
and a putrid cycle repeats itself.

What happens when you catch yourself dead in life?
Existing for others, but not for yourself?

What happens when you catch a glance of you in the mirror
and the people who claim to know you so well
are all wrong?

Lay down
It is not sin to stare too long at space until your head clears.
It is not sin to turn thoughts around in your head until the
empty ones dissipate.
It's not cruelty to daydream as the sun shines.
It's respite for your soul, for your spirit, for your body.

It is the fresh air in your lungs.
And it is your Creator's desire
that you find pleasure not only in the work of your hands
but in the limpness of your body;
when your spirit departs temporarily
to a place unremembered.
— 20/Oct/22.

22

Jonathan[7]

Lord, direct me.
Bring to my front
the opportunity that is for me.

Direct me to who to speak to.
Fill my bosom with godly friends,
that their wisdom
may soften my hardened heart.

Let their hands direct me to Your Face.
Let their voices direct me to Your Gaze.
Let it—
Calm my soul
Speak ancient wisdom to my spirit
Tell me what to do.
— 07/Jan/24.

7 1 Samuel 18:1.

23

World stop

I wish the world would stop
When I'm hurting.
But if it did
what kind of world would I find
when my hurt is healed?

Can a halted world
heal my wound?
Wouldn't a halted world
make everyone else sick like me?

For life is progressive
and to live is to move;
whether in success or failure.
Backwards or forward;
in sickness or health.

Then everything that stops is *anti-life*;
or as we know it more intimately, death.
— 27/Dec/23.

24

Ruby

Worried about many things,
yet one is necessary.
It cannot be taken away, this thing;
it is precious like a ruby.

Come, let us reason together;
what lies at the core of the things you seek?
After they've made you happy or sad, whatever;
they steal your time, hear the clock tick.

But there is a certain business
that comes with an eternal reward.
It does not leave you in uneasiness
if you decide to be its steward.

It seems to restore time,
giving you a fail-safe to thrive.
It costs, but not a dime;
you have to pay with your life.

If you desire profit,
this is where it is never devalued.
If from life's vanity, you desire an exit,
this is where all earthly things are touched by heaven,
renewed.

And where is *here*? Here is where,
seeking the Master's Will to accomplish it;
for He never gives more than you can bear.
Embrace the Spirit, so your flesh takes a hit.

For the one who sets his love on God
has set aside corruption.
He will live forever.
— 16/Jan/24.

25

Stay

Won't you stay?
Don't run away from Him
when your heart is not fully mended.
He is closer than it would seem,
making whole what was tainted.

Won't you stay?
There are unsettled torrents within you.
Gloomy and dark clouds around you.
But when He enters, that's darkness' cue.
Peace and rest, that's what you're due.

Won't you stay?
All is well that ends well.
And if it is not well, it is not the end.
Time will tell, time will tell;
those who wait on the Lord will excel.

Won't you stay?
You're watching the time

but He's watching you.
    A million other things to do,
    notifications chime,
    but how will your heart be, when it is through?

Won't you stay?
No patient rushes the physician.
And this One treats not just body, but soul and spirit.
        You will know when you are healed,
        and not by the passage of time;
        your heart will beat again, in love,
        and joy will be pumped through
        your veins.

Whenever we worship God from our hearts
there is a release in our spirit.
Every heaviness is lifted.
— 21/Dec/23.

26

Epitaph

Today, I am in mourning.
This is my epitaph.
To something that never was
but I thought could be.

The Lord had said
If *My Grace is there, it'll flourish.*
So I went ahead with my works
and maybe crushed the seed,
that needed time and patience,
with excessive tendering and petting.
Are the petals falling?

Now my heart is broken.
Not by anyone but me.
I went too far, too fast
with one who wasn't even on the journey.
In pain, I must pull myself back.
In hurt, I will wipe my tears.

What else is there to do but move on?
It is not faith but foolishness
to cast pearls before swine[8].

Abba, Father,
I have come to the end of myself.
I know what I want and I won't settle.
For the heart of a king is in Your hand[9];
have Your Way.

And maybe not here,
not with this one.
But someday, somewhere
I'll be found by my *one*.
I will see, that I wasn't asking for too much
in wanting one, whose desires for me and such
will be plain, open, discernible.
Whose words will be backed by action, tangible.

I honour Your Design, Abba,
for one that will lead
and Your Will be done.
— 30/Dec/23.

8 Matthew 7:6-7.
9 Proverbs 21:1.

27

Man your post

Man your post.
Protect your coast.
The hurt will come, the shame and ridicule,
but if He tells you to stand, it is for your good.

The value of the *kingdom*
is measured in souls.
If we lose our guard when our souls go dim
on our heavenly mandate, it'll take a toll.

Yes, Abba has many soldiers,
and deliverance will come, from one place or another—
But what tragedy of a man rejects God's Plea?
What hardness of heart abandons the ministry of reconciliation?

There is not affliction worse than unbelief.
If a man is saved, he has all he needs.
But the one without Christ,
Yahweh yearns for him.

If He never leaves the one behind
            How should we?
If one man is sufficient to stand in the gap
            Why can't we?
— 12/Jan/24.

28

A stream

The Lord has opened up a stream
of worship within me
to adore Him.
I am not worthy.

I am unworthy of You, my Lord

Who am I?

Nothing before the men of the world
but everything to You.

You have opened my heart to hear Your Voice.
Strengthened my hand to do Your Work.
Blessed my obedience to be manifest
in the sight of men.
My heart cowers before You in meekness.

Who am I?

I am nobody that You should lead me so.
He called me son, priest, friend, child, beloved;
the apple of His eyes, His workmanship.

He sees my little strength and blesses it.
He sees disaster ahead and redirects me.
He watches me, day and night,
keeping my tears in His bottle.
None has fallen without His notice.
I see all my inconsistencies and failings.
He sees a warrior and a priest.
I bu amama amasi amasi[10];
        There is no end to You.

Lion and the Lamb;
You are my Lord and life.
I live for You.
I will die than let You go.
With every iota of me, I will hold on to You.

Yet my confidence is not in my strength.
        For can a child hold on to their Father?
My Father's Grip is my anchor.
If You do nothing more, You have done enough.
        What place is better, than the Shadow of the
        Almighty[11]?
— 22/Dec/23.

10 Igbo praise chant mostly rendered to God which loosely translates to 'You are beyond comprehension, or there is no end to knowing You, or You are the one that we cannot know completely'.
11 Psalm 91:1.

29

God's green

Is the world only beautiful when it makes us happy?
And depressing when it steals our hopes?

Is nature only beautiful when she's agreeable?
The sun's rays are welcome when you want warmth
but scorching when your skin desires the cool?

If you could only see that nature remains mostly stable
and notice that the major variable is you.
If only you could see that the universe and its laws
are held up in place by the sheer will of Him
and that you're the one allowed to have a choice
not just react to stimuli.

Then maybe you would lose your speech
when a complaint arises in your throat.
Stiffen your fist before you
shake it at the pattering rain.
Loosen your brows before a frown
forms to steal the happiness in your cheeks.

Maybe you would look into yourself
to calm the storm brooding within
before it spills over
and darkens the world without.
— 19/Oct/22.

30

Bleed

One day, a knife poked my heart.
It ran deep and I bled terribly.
But the blood was black
and the taste, bitter as death.

The one who drove the knife
was a dear friend;
hurt by the betrayal,
unforgiveness was born and bloomed.

When I woke, 'how could he?'
When I prayed, 'how could he?'
When I worked, 'how could he?'
When I inhaled, 'how could he?'

And so a cage was created.
I locked myself in.
The keys nestled in my palm
but I would not open.
For 'how could he?'

My Lord was watching,
watching me bleed unceasingly.
He knocked.
He was here to fix me.

I fidgeted.
He knocked.
I shook.
He knocked again.

And when my eyes finally met my Master's,
His Gaze holding mine;
I crumbled in a heap of healing.
The door flung open.

'How could he?' I shrieked.
My humiliation, anger and hurt pouring out.
My hurt had pumped the ugly blood.
The bitter blood drained

My Lord stooped to meet me.
With a gentle finger,
He lifted my head;
and my gaze to meet His.

It was electric, His Touch.
It was healing, His Gaze.
It was empowering, His Presence.
My heart became quiet.

Without a word, He forgave me.
            How could I not forgive?
To the one who never knew the depth
of the hurt he caused me, I said
'I forgive you.'

Oh the words hurt, stung.
It seemed to drive the knife deeper
but then it fell out.
For my bitterness had been keeping it in place.

I accepted my Lord's Desire
and strength returned to my heart.
Then I stood and walked out of my prison,
for a light that wasn't there, appeared to lead me home.
— 21/Dec/23.

31

Bended knees

When I go through temptations and trials
you help me persevere.
Your Word says nothing will tempt me
more than I can bear.

When I lack and have nothing but needs,
You come through, reassuring me with words
of Your previous Deeds.

When my flesh seems to win
and I feel guilt drown me in endless sorrows;
I remember the bruises You bore to save me.
And now I come to You on bended knees

Break me, heal me, mould me into a vessel fit to carry your glory
And I will carry
the Gospel of Your Goodness

wherever I go
as l o n g as You tarry.
— 16/Jun/21.

32

Okwu nzuzu

Onye n'ekwu otutu okwu
agaghi agbanari okwu asi
N'ihi na osiri ike ikwu otutu eziokwu n'ime otutu okwu

Otutu okwu diri ndi uche ha na alahu ura
Nakwa ndi n'ege uche ha nti
karia ige ihe mmuo ha na gwa ha nke bu eziokwu.

Foolish talk

One who speaks excessively
cannot keep from spewing lies.
For it is hardly possible to state *too many truths in too many words.*

Many words are for those who have put their *minds to sleep.*
And who cherish the tingling of their senses
over the *awakening* of their spirit.
— 20/Oct/22.

33

There is grace

There is grace for me;
the kind that levels the playing field.
There is grace abounding
and it's not about who I know
or where I've been.

This grace calls my name.
I knew nothing, didn't merit a claim.
'*But He knows you*', grace calls again.
I dropped the heavy yoke that covered me in pain.

Now I have set my love upon Him.
For this love is more wondrous than it would seem.
Another sheep He has delivered.
O let His Name be revered!
— 29/Dec/23.

34

Finding time

Yesterday I woke up and I was 18.
Today I'm 21.
My heart clenches in fear;
it sings in the notes of unachieved dreams.
I wonder where the time has gone.

As I brush my teeth, I resolve to find time.
The mirror reveals my tired eyes;
I head out, 'I won't be back till I find it.'
On my way out:

I meet a *lover,* I meet a *friend;* I get my heart broken.
I get it fixed up, not quite the same but enough to love again.
I hold a bottle of water to the sun in my toil
and a glass of wine to the moon in my ecstasy.

I *fall,* I *kneel,* I *stand,* I fall *again.*
Many bruises I wear and many more away from what I seek.
I meet religion; I meet lies.
I meet Christ, I see truth;

and when I hold it in my hands, it does not leak;
or escape so slowly that I barely notice until it is gone.

Now time stands still; I *found* it.
I revel in its ticks and tocks.
And when I dance with my Lover, it is without care.
How can I hurry, when eternity is in me, here?
— 13/Apr/22.

35

A quiet time contemplation

The giver, the taker;
giving us His Blessings
taking away what stands in His Way
of becoming the centre of our world.

Kind and loving Father,
King over all.
God the Son cleanses
His blood making an eternal pact
that grants us true freedom.

At the Cross He bled
          to prevent us from being led
                    down the broad road by the evil one.

Glory to Him
now and forever more!
May His Name be praised

in the heavens and all the earth.
May His Spirit ever dwell in us.
— 26/May/21.

36

Last minute

I can tell why Abba loves the last minute;
the miracles of the eleventh hour.
It is at that point, often,
that every ounce of self is gone;
like dead petals on a once pretty flower.

We stop depending on 'I'.
We've run out of options.
The *mighty man of battle* loves His Glory,
He will not share it.

We stop looking within
and instead, give it all to Him.
Our hands are empty;
every end, a dead one.

Who have we on earth beside Him?
Who in heaven but Him?

For the end of man
is the beginning of God.
And when all hope is lost
is when the Living Hope shows up.

Our eyes will see the glory of the Lord.
Our lips will brim and spill with thanksgiving.
The victorious one
has given me victory.
Amen.
— 21/Dec/23.

37

Echi echi

Odi n'ihu, adighi anya di ka anyi si eche
O bu echi—
echi agbakunyere echi ibe ya
Echi ga ma mma
ma oburu na i kwua ugwo taa taa juru n'aka gi

Ma mgbe echi ahu i na tu anya ya biara
ka o hapu ibia kute gi n'ime mma kwara—
ka ihapu i bu onye ji ugwo
mgbe i kwesiri ino na-eri ulu ihe echi wetara

Maka na echi anaghi adigide
Na o na-asapu di ka mmiri no na nkpusi aka
Ozokwa, ka m chetara gi na idighi iche ebe ndi ozo no
ndu gi adighi iche na ndu ndi ozo
Ma oburu na anyi me mgbe anyi nwere ka oburu mgbe di iche
ka ma i me ka agaasi na ihe anyi nwere ime di mkpa karia ndu na onwe ya
Otu odi, echi a bia go, ma na kwa.

Tomorrow tomorrow

The future is not far as we think.
It is tomorrow—
a bunch of tomorrows.
And tomorrow can only be good
if you pay the dues today asks of you.

But when that tomorrow
you have been waiting on
dawns,
let it be without regrets—
so you're not a debtor
when you should be enjoying tomorrow's pleasures.

For tomorrow is fleeting
and it slips through fingers like water.
Once again, you're reminded how *ordinary* you are,
how *ordinary* life is,
when we make moments special—
rather than life itself.
Now tomorrow has come and *gone.*
— 30/Dec/23.

38

A new dawn

A new dawn.
More laughs, more joy.
More rest.
The Lord is contending with anything
that comes for my peace.

A joy without an earthly source
from The One that makes my heart leap.
My Lord makes me blush
like a shy bride
when I think of His Goodness

His Love lights up my soul.
His Presence revives my spirit.
His Word brings vitality to my temple.

When He seems far
I sit and remember
His Rescue and His Goodness.
But this God has never failed me;

I hold His Word
like a thread my life hangs on to.
If I leave Him, where do I go?
Will the world ever be an alternative?

His Business is my business.
Knowing that I am His is a joy
that my heart cannot fathom or contain.
Knowing that He is mine, too,
living in me, His Temple.

I don't just know a king.
I know THE King.
And He is my Father,
my own Abba.

I can speak to Him, here and now
and He will hear me.
He will answer me;
hide me in light so
the darkness cannot decipher me.

The barks of a million dogs
cannot stop a caravan's journey.
I am in the Lord's caravan.

My future is safe and beautiful.
I do not think much about tomorrow.
Only today's evil, I focus on.

My Lord knows and that is enough for me.
He keeps every promise to me.
I ask and my joy is full.

He does not let me stray
or wallow in my misery.
He corrects me with coincidences;
returning my attention to Him in
mysterious, creative ways.

To have a Father that listens
and moves in my favour and honour—
What a joy!
Let *all of me* worship You.
— 08/Jan/24.

39

Void

What is this void that makes my heart ache?
What emptiness that silences my song?
Saddens my eyes, slows my pace?
Droops my head, shakes my core?

'What is wrong?'
'I don't know,' but my eyes fill with tears.
'What is wrong?'
'I don't know' but my lips tremble.
Aching to howl and wail
like it is the end of the world
or maybe just the end of mine.

Loneliness cuts me.
To whom will my speech not be a burden?
Who will acknowledge my silence?

Who will become '*nkem*[12]'
truly, in every way?

What if he never comes
since I was made for God and not man?
Can I fill this space with family and friends and purpose
and be complete?
Since I was made alone: for God and not man?

Can I trust that he will come?
Can I trust God if he never does?
I have no desire to be a Eunuch.
Praise Christ, hail Paul!
Not me.

Unlike heaven, a man is not a goal.
A man cannot be found.
And have I been hiding in the wrong places?
Or is it not yet time?
— 27/Dec/23.

12 Igbo word and expression which loosely translates as 'mine' or 'my own'. Used affectionately for a person who is valued and deeply admired. Nearly synonymous with English expressions like 'sweetheart' or 'darling'.

40

N'enu ihe omumu

Aka m no na amu ka m hu Chukwu n'anya
di ka o si hu m n'anya

Aka m no na amu ka oburu ihe mbu
ma na enu ma n'akuku n'ime ndu m

Aka m no na amu ka m kwado obi m
di ka ihu onyinye m ge nye Chukwu
we debe ya n'ukwu ya kwa ubochi

Aka m no na amu ka m hapu i jide si ike
k'agaasi na mu elugo ebe m na aga
N'ihi na, n'ebe akagha aga no du n'ihu ka na-abia
Obu ihe mara nnukwu mma, mu na Nna m ino—
o na ato obi m uto nke ukwuu.

Still learning

Still learning to love God
as much as He loves me.

Still learning to put Him first
above and beyond.

Still learning to wrap my heart like a present
each day, and drop it at His Feet.

Still learning not to hold on too tightly
because there is more to go and more to come.
It's beautiful being with Abba,
I am basking.
— 19/Dec/21.

41

All things beautiful

He makes everything beautiful
in His time.[13]
The time I have waited
has cost me nothing but my weakness.

The end thereof is beauty and strength.
I am delighted in the ways of my Yahweh
even if I might not always understand them.

Why should I compare?
Isn't that to accuse my Abba of favouritism
when He loves His children equally;
and His Plans for me are not the same for you?

Weep with me as I rejoice with you.
Let us deepen our trust in Him;
on hills and in valleys,

13 Ecclesiastes 3:11.

through all seasons,
He remains the hero of our story.
— 29/Dec/23.

42

Sometimes

Sometimes, it is a loud shout
to disturb the neighbours.
Sometimes, it is a sweet sonorous sound
that calls others to join in.

Sometimes, it is gut-wrenching sobs
with no audible words.
Sometimes, it is endless laughter
like the Holy Spirit is a comedian.

Sometimes, it is the sound of war
casting down imaginations and high things.
Sometimes, it is the silent tears
wetting dry skin.

Sometimes, it is contemplative silence
ready to receive from the Throne room.
Sometimes, it is a melody of thanksgiving

with dancing as David did[14].

Sometimes it is a conversation,
spirit to Spirit.

Sometimes, it is an upward glance
bidding: Lord, *come.*

Sometimes, it is a waiting
and we cannot move until He does.
Sometimes, it is empty silence, a numb mind;
a heavy heart and muted, unmoving lips.

Sometimes, it is fatigue
because our temples don't feel quite right.
Sometimes, it is the movement of a pen
pouring out words we cannot speak.

Sometimes, it is a feast on His Words
examining ourselves in that mirror.
Sometimes, it is a roving mind
with distracted and scattered thoughts.

Sometimes, it is a starry-eyed wonder
feasting on the beauty of our God.
Sometimes, it is petition upon petition—
Who will the child ask if not the Father?

---

14 2 Samuel 6:14.

Whatever it may be;
He understands it
He welcomes it

Brokenness has many forms and shapes
and today's form might not be tomorrow's
But as long as we always
find our way back to our knees

Bring our hearts to worship
and use our lives to obey
We'll find Him there,
waiting, ready to touch us from heaven
over and again.
— 29/Dec/23.

Come unto me, all ye that labour and are heavy laden, and I will give you rest. Take my yoke upon you, and learn of me; for I am meek and lowly in heart: and ye shall find rest unto your souls. For my yoke is easy, and my burden is light.
- Matthew 11:28-30

43

For Damini, my damsel

You are:
Counsel that uplifts my soul;
the wonderful scent of freshly plucked roses,
glue that holds me together when I fall apart.

You are:
the cheerleader that makes the game worth it.
A bubble to hide in when the world scares me;
patient ears that don't tire to listen.

You are:
the brightest light on a gloomy day;
a poise of peace that sends the storm away,
a beautiful enchantment of priceless things.

You are all these things
yet so much more...
— 14/Feb/24.

44

Thinking deeply

I like to think deeply about my feelings;
why do I feel this way?
Pour out my thoughts;
what fears feed my mind?
What motivates my soul,
steering it on this path?

To marinate in silence;
a tool of truth and discovery
revealing what was hidden.
Diving into deep waters
to provoke a treasure
that will last the test of time.
— 30/Dec/23.

45

Surprise party

Every morning, I wake up to You
and a day You have set up for me;
like a surprise party
for an unaware celebrant.

It's a celebration every day, with You.
My day is littered with gift boxes, big and small
of miracles, a million little miracles.
I open one after another.

I shriek with excitement
sending a tear-filled glance at You;
'You didn't have to,' I whisper.
'Of course I had to,' You whisper back.

And when the day comes to an end
Just when I think the party's over
You send me to bed with a warm kiss
I rest in Your Embrace.

As You fill my sleep with dreams of Your Promises,
there are more surprises lurking
at the edge of my awakening.
— 08/Oct/21.

46

Lethal

A lethal dose of courage
and an equal one of love
to enter this new year; a new page
in a new book, a mystery to solve.

What will tomorrow bring?
New friendships, challenges, solutions?
I have no fear, only a tinge;
I am living this life for generations.

Men and women will come after me
and I'll tell what a special year '24 was.
Oh I'll spill the tea
that the elephant didn't die without a fuss.

But it was expected
and I came prepared
I have died my death and all that's left is life;

call me a cat, but it was the elephant's first time.
— 01/Jan/24.

P.S. - For context, an elephant represents new challenges. I got it from this quote: '*Let the young man in his desperation go out and hunt. If he kills the elephant, his poverty ends. If the elephant kills him, his poverty ends.*' It hardened my resolve to do challenging things in 2024.

47

Weighty words

I know we say these words often:
the Lord is merciful, the Lord is kind;
but let us not neglect the weight they carry
or that our daily reality is hinged on them—
The Lord is good, the Lord is faithful.

For He holds our lives in His hands
Giving our lungs its breath
and our hearts their beats
If He wasn't, we wouldn't be
Like the clay would never be
without the Potter.

Let these words provoke
deep thought and gratitude and obedience
Let them make our hearts dance and our hands do
while spirit rejoices
The Lord is mighty, mighty in battle;
our safety is assured.

And when our enemies gather, the Lord laughs
It is a comedy show
where fire burns and blood flows.
— 30/Dec/23.

48

Ubochi ufodu

Ubochi ufodu n'ejuputa na ihe n'enye obi anwuri
Mgbe ufodu ubochi ufodu anaghi acho ka
enwe ihe ga enye ha nsogbu

Ubochi ufodu, anyi na-acho ka ndi ozo nuo ihe anyi n'ekwu
Ubochi ufodu kwa anyi anaghi acho ka anu onu anyi
n'ihi na nkpotu di n'ime isi anyi bu ihe n'ada uda

Ubochi ufodu, anyi n'enwe mmasi igaghari
Ubochi ufodu anyi ekpebie ino ofu ebe

Ubochi ufodu, anyi di ndu n'etiti ndi di ndu
Ubochi dum ndi ozo, anyi bu ndi nwuru anwu.

Some days

Some days are filled with ecstatic exuberance;
others carry a quiet energy that
wishes not to be disturbed.

On some days we want to speak and be heard;
other days we will not utter a sound
for the thoughts in our heads are loud enough.

On some days we move…
On other days we stay.

On some days we live
and every other day we don't, we die.
— Apr/2022.

49

My heart has written

My mind is seated in peace
My heart is soaked in stability
I wasn’t looking
but I found something, Someone, perfect.

He makes my heart swell with the purest rhythms of life
My mouth does not know how to express.

In that lonely place,
where I become a stranger to myself;
He fights the enemies I cannot see
and the ones I see, He has let slip through
to strengthen me.

For every ‘yes’ I say, a thousand rewards
And for every ’no’, a thousand mercies.

I cry out, ‘I am undeserving’
He whispers, ‘You’re a son’
I cry out, ‘I am not worthy’

He whispers, 'I have made you whole'
I protest, 'I am filthy'
He replies, 'I am not, what is mine is yours'

So I dust myself as He raised me by my hand and heart;
Lifted; all of me. Lifted.
An end to that bow of defeat and shame;
that hiding of head and face.
His Face shone on mine and His Light entered the depths of my soul I'd never been to
Lifted; all of me. Lifted.

So I pledged the life He gave me *back* to Him;
He who sings songs of commitment and loyalty over me.
He is like colour in a black-and-white world, prospering my soul.

My Abba, my Father, my Lover.
As long as my hands are raised in worship of You
I have victory.
— 11/Apr/23.

50

Ekperem

Ekperem anaghi ada na nti ochi
Mba, obunadi ma otu
Echiche m, ihe n'esogbum, ihe ndi natu m ujo
Ihe ndi a nine Chukwu mazuru ha

Mgbe ufodu, ona azam ngwa-ngwa
ome ka m kue ime ofuma
Mgbe ufodu ona ete aka
ma na udo nke Chineke na-adi n'ime m
Mgbe ufodu aziza ekperem anaghi abia
ma ihe ka mma na-abia n'onodu ya

K'osinadi, ana m atukwasi Chineke Onye nwem obi mgbe nine
Aga m enye ya otito
N'ihi n'ihunanya ya nadi ohuru n'ututu obuna
Ikwesi ntukwasi obu ya nadi kwa ohuru abani obuna.

My prayers

My prayers do not fall on deaf ears;
    No, not one.
My thoughts, my worries, my fears;
    No, not one.

Sometimes, He answers so quickly
    it takes my breath away.
Sometimes, it takes a while
    but He keeps my peace.
Sometimes, it never comes
    but something better does.

Whatever the case may be
I will trust the Lord, my God
I will praise Him
His Loving-kindness abounds every morning
and His Faithfulness every night.
— 29/Dec/23.

51

The Word

Here is a cure-all:
I cannot describe how much the Bible helps me.

When I'm sick, I find my *healing* there
When I lack, I find my *needs* met
When I have been shockingly foolish, I find *wisdom and correction* there
When I have erred, I find *forgiveness* there

When the world takes from me, the Word gives to me
When I'm in despair, I find mysterious peace there
In this life, I find my purpose there
and when I die, I will find my eternity there.
— 31/Mar/22.

52

Roses are red

Roses are red
Violets are blue
I'm in sync with You
and I'll do all You'll have me do

Roses are red
Violets are blue
Fast or slow may seem this race
but I'll always move at Your Pace.
— 10/Jan/22.

53

Legacy

I am certain the Lord has
a legacy for me.

Lift up my head to meet Your gaze
Lighten my heart to contain You

Once there was a girl
who knew of a God
That He was seated in the heavens
and sometimes He answered her prayers
Other times, she simply figured things out.

She believed, but not enough to change her
She loved, but not enough to fully surrender
She trusted, but she liked being realistic *too*
for the times when He went silent on her
She did not understand Him
or the entirety of His Love for her.

She thought He played a part in her life
She did not know He was her life,

not intimately;
In some ways, she was blind.

So, one day, He got up from His throne
and descended among humanity
On her door, He knocked
She barely heard the knock
He stood waiting
There was a party inside
The music was loud.

One day, the music stopped
A fight broke out and she started to bleed
She stepped out for a plaster
but the Chief Physician was at her door
with the same countenance as when He first knocked:
'Let me heal you'

She fell into His embrace
The pain oozed out of her
Out with all the lies she'd believed about Him
She started to see Him in her past
All the places she thought He'd disappointed her;
where she'd thought that He couldn't be trusted.

She saw her rebellion
She had known He could be trusted
but she wanted options, to be safe, incase.
Incase He left her,

even though she was the one who left.

How do you love with logic
Someone who loves you without logic?
How do you give a part of you
to Someone who gave not just what He had
but all of Him?
How can you hold back the gift of you
from Him who stepped down to be with you?

Her realism was in error
It was doubt masquerading.
And once there was a confession
there began an ascension.
For anyone who partners with Yahweh
who has no options outside Him;
such a man lives above
this world and everything in it.

Worldly men fight to be remembered after they're passed
Yahweh writes the legacy of His children
In the stars, like Abraham[15];
On the cross, like Jesus[16].

If anyone seeks immortality
Let Him seek God and walk with Him

---

15 Genesis 15:5.
16 Matthew 27:42.

And if the only thing known about us
is that we walked with Him, as Enoch[17]—
let that be enough.
— 11/Jan/24.

17 Genesis 5:24.

54

A Circle and a square

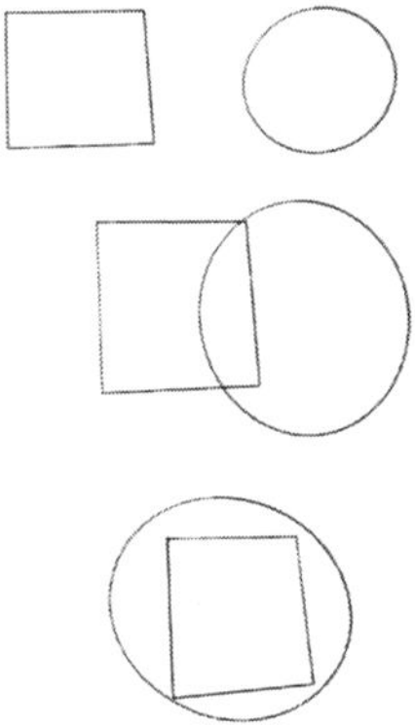

I don't always say the right things
Sometimes I am a circle
when the hole in your chest is a square
I am not enough.

I have words when you need music
Advice when you need silence
Absent when you need my presence
I am not enough.

My lack comes from within me
I cannot give what I do not have
Sometimes I am not what you need
Sometimes I fear I am not your only option

But then I am glad I am not
I wish you find happiness everywhere
Even if it is not with me
I have nothing to prove

When I fail you in this way
I will go on my knees again
to ask the One who is Love
to teach me to love you.
— 14/Feb/24.

55

Dead girl

Let me be the difference
Let me be the one to bring Jesus to mind
Let me keep shut against the popular rhythms in the air
Let me be '*spiri-coco*[18]'
Let me not watch the popular movies
because my Lord would not enjoy it
I look out for my Lord's Life in me—
I am a dead girl[19].

Let me be the difference
Let it always be '*that deep*' for me
Let me flee from every appearance of evil
Let it never be '*just vibes*' for me
For I am not foolish, I know what my Lord wants

---

18 Expression which hints on the person being spiritual perhaps to a fault in the eyes of the addresser.
19 A derogatory term used to describe a young lady who is devoted to living life by the terms of spiritual and moral codes of GOD. Kindly, also, refer to 2 Corinthians 5:15.

It is a vessel unto honour;
untainted, unblemished, and uncommon.

So, let me do all these things
It is an uncommon life
as my Lord desires—
I live to please my Lord.
— 22/Dec/23.

56

Youth

Strength, vitality, adventure
Foolishness, myopia, naivety
A time to do it all
but why do I feel so small?
I stand in the middle
of the beginning and the end.

I tried everything that I could
I died and lived in many ways
I was the wise and the foolish
The prophet and a sinner
An adult and a child
A conservative and a nonconformist—
And I prepared to give an account of each
to my Creator.
– 2022.

57

Assurance

My heart has an assurance:
it sits in tranquillity
like a baby with its mother
Whether the earth is moved
Whether He comes or tarries
Whether I live or die
I am filled with joy, irrespective

Daily He seals my fate
I am resigned to whatever He has for me
He goes before me
I stay close behind
Abiding in His Shadow

I have confidence in nothing else
Dear friend, put your hope in nothing else
but the One that does not change
Not in money that grows wings to fly
or people that may lose the light
or in events that may not hold

Hinge your future on Him
Take no note of the finer details
For our God is a master artist
A painter with the most beautiful strokes

I dwell in security and hope
because I sit with Yeshua—
The One who has conquered the world.
— 08/Jan/24.

58

No more

Why has my heart
gone looking for trouble?
I did not greet my Daddy
I went to my Mac

On the screen, I saw
problems I could not face
without first facing my Lord

I must remember
That when I pray, fastening my gaze on Him
He works, acting on my behalf

So, no more toiling
He gives me these things
while I sleep.
— 09/Feb/24.

59

Restored

My Abba has restored my soul;
the itchy hands of anxiety thought to snatch it.
Lord Jesus has restored my peace;
a thousand worries clouded my thoughts.

All I could say was 'Jesus help me'
and He did—
Even when I had no praise to render,
and no song to offer
He heard the language of my tears.

What mercy!
Truly, I have a Father that never fails:
Who kept me trusting
when the odds were against me.
Who kept my heart in its place
in Him.

Now my testimony is manifest—
The Lord has given me good health;

even the doctors agree!
My tears have ceased.
My heart leaps.

God has kept me
'Don't you remember the plans I have for you?
I will satisfy you with long life[20]
I remember, my Lord
Forgive my anxiety
Forgive my unbelief

Truly the Lord is in heaven
and I on earth—
I will let my words be few.
— 29/Dec/23.

20 Psalm 91:16.

60

~~Bated~~ breath(e)

No more bated breath, breathe.
How can I live in the future
when the Lord is in my present?

No more personal proposals
No more desires birthed from conformity
Let my God speak and my God alone
    No more suggestions
    Only Your directions

If He won't move
I won't move
Even if the world quakes
My only dream is You

Decision by decision,
each passing through You,
I will come to total dependence on You

No more dreams, goals, ambitions.

Not for me. What do I know?
Not enough.
They say if you are not where you want to be
then you do not know enough
I surrender my independence to the one Who knows it all

I surrender this vessel
Take it and fill it as You will
Truly, I surrender
See, my hands are empty—
save for what You have put in it
per time

Let me see what kind of life it'll be
if I never move until He gives the word.
Let me see what He will make of me,
if obedience was all I could afford.
— 22/Feb/24.

61

Maybe

How do we go to bed, every day
with such confidence that we will see the next sunrise?
What if the world ends, what if the moon dies?
What if the sun gets upset, what if dawn would rather not break?
What if our bodies become an enemy to life?

There are thoughts which we will not think
not because we're scared, or because they are untrue
but because the evidence of life seems more
overwhelming than the evidence of it's sinister twin

So, maybe I will die
but I didn't die yesterday
So, maybe I won't tomorrow
All the people I woke up with the day before
I still saw yesterday, too

In a world where life is hope
maybe is the motto.
— 17/Oct/22.

62

Yahweh Sabaoth

When He steps in, every darkness steps out;
He is mighty, my own goodness.
My heart thirsts for You,
my mind cannot understand You
but I want You beyond what I could ever know.

Almighty Jesus, please hear me:
        close every gap between us
        clear every distance that keeps me from You.
My heart cannot contain You
so my mouth keeps pouring out;
about your wondrous performances,
about your endless loyalty to me.

My mind is filled with thoughts of You:
        I want You, Jesus
        I want You, Holy Ghost
        I want You, Abba
Take me and make me yours completely;
there's no one else's I'd rather be.

Be jealous for me as I am desperate for You;
fill me Jesus, feed me—
I have no source but You.

I lay awake thinking of You.
I drift off to sleep praying to dream of You.
Lord Jesus, my Bridegroom,
I long for You.
Mighty are You, the world under Your feet.
— 14/Dec/23.

63

Sweet like Kola

A love that is chosen,
it grows on you.
A person with flaws
that you have accepted.
— 26/Jan/14.

I want to hold your laughter:
        Keep it in a bottle—
        Few drops in my moisturizer
        so it stays on my face;
        maybe adds a bloom to my cheeks.

I want some in my jollof rice
        so I feel it on my tongue and teeth;
        maybe it affects my laughter
        as it goes down my throat.

I want some in my bag
        so I can take a peep
when my day goes awry;
maybe it restores some hope.

I want some in my spray bottle
so the scent of joy stays on me.

I would not want to record it
to play it after;
For I've often wondered
how something so beautiful
could sound so ugly.
— 04/Feb/24.

P.S. - When I wrote the first stanza, I knew it was incomplete. I don't like to force my poetry so I left it to marinate. One night, I was talking and laughing with my little sister and I felt joy bubble within me, threatening to explode in my chest, just because of that moment spent doing what sisters do. I asked her, calling her name first, '{redacted}, why is laughter so ugly?' After which I proceeded to alter my laughter to make it sound a bit cuter but it flopped terribly and we burst out laughing the ugliest peals of laughter I have ever heard to date. This poem is a tribute to this moment and many more that God has given me through the irreplaceable people He's surrounded me with.

I wrote the first stanza initially thinking about romantic love. But in the moment where I experienced my sister's beautiful and ugly laughter and it stood out to me so that I had to document it, I knew that family and friendship might be the greatest love from humans that I will ever know.

64

N'enigwe

Ukwu m di n'uwa
ma obi m no n'enigwe

Mgbe obuna ndi ilo m kporo aha m
Nna m n'eji oku aza ha.

In heaven

My feet on earth but
my heart is in heaven

When my enemies call me
my Father answers with fire.
— 24/Dec/23.

65

I see Him

I'll admit it's not always rosy:
Sometimes the sun shines so brightly
We see the moon at 6 PM
The breeze gently sways our hair, our clothes, maybe us
He is certainly here!
Our hearts leap.

But sometimes, there is a bond between our eyelids,
the bond of tears
and it shuts everything out but the pain.

Can we still see Him *then*?
Can we See Him *waiting*?
Can we see Him *ordering* our steps?
Can we see Him *clap* at our little wins?
Can we see Him *beam*, like a proud Father
that we have made Him?

See Him clean your tears
See Him comfort you

It may not be a vivid picture, but it is clear enough
for you to see Him
See Him reaching for you
See you safe in Him.
— 19/Dec/21.

66

Flawed

They're raving and raging
Their lips are moving
Their fists, punching the air
Eye sockets, bulging

Rancour fills the air
Bile chokes me
Bitterness is sweet
in the ears of blind men

Now they're looking at me
They want my lips to move
I will do no such thing
Their gazes are threatening

The prisoner before me shudders
His head is shrunk low
He waits for judgement from my lips
He expects nothing less

But how can I?
When in this man, I see myself?
How can I?
When I can barely see
through the log in my eye
How can I?
What makes me more righteous than he?
Because I have done my bad deeds in secret?
And this man was not so lucky
for his evil deeds fell on the day of the owner[21]

There is but one sickness that plagues men
Race, class, social status cannot change it
The sickness of sin
makes me no different from this man

So I keep quiet
For I can barely see this man before me
All I see, are my bloodstained hands and
black, black heart
All I can see are my dirty deeds and if I dare point a finger,
four times that number points back at me

And I'll be guilty
guilty of them all.
— 26/Apr/22.

---

21 This is in reference to the Nigerian Adage, '**Everyday Is For The Thief, One Day Is For The Owner**' illustrating the concept of fairness and justice in the long run.

67

Bless the day

I bless the day You
walked into my life.
I bless Your patience
in waiting for me.

You have shown me things
too heavy for human eyes.
You have filled me
with the awe and fear of You.
I have carried instructions
too beautiful for my soul;
pieces of the Will of God
have been completed through my hands.

He watches everything that concerns me;
that hair that fell out of my lashes
this morning, He knows.
I am so honoured that I met You,
I am blessed among the living.

My heart beats in rhythm with Yours.
Generating love, my being radiates peace.
I am so content I could cry.
The One outside time
has favoured me in time.

When I think of You, Jesus
nothing compares.
You who stoops to conquer;
You have broken my walls.
I love You Jesus, I do.
You have given me a portion
that I have not worked for;
posting my reward to heavenly places.

So many requests on my mind
But all that pours out of my lips is 'thanks'.
That I can complain and be restless
is because Your Breath resides within me.

Can the dead grumble?
Can the dead sing a song?

If I had to choose
I would give thanks to Your Name

Alaye lo ma yi o
O ku ka le yi o[22]
Let my life worship You
Let my pen exalt You

Whatever supplications I have
He answers first with peace.
Or does He not know what I need
before I ask for it?

Instead make me Your vessel
on hand to serve You.
Send me to Your lost sons and daughters,
let me live the life You designed for me.

If You answer my material requests
even more will emanate—
In this corrupt world, there is no end to these things.

But if You would make me Yours
Fully and truly
Generations will call me blessed
They will trace revival to me
and they will see what the Lord does
with the one who trusts Him.
— 12/Jan/24.

---

22 Yoruba praise chant to God meaning 'It is when I'm alive I can praise You; In death I cannot praise You'.

68

Simple

To walk with Jesus is simple
Only if we listen to the Word, not men
For men have a way of complicating things
but if we know Jesus, He simplifies them.

Ask, and you will receive[23]
And if you don't see it, keep asking
Considering time, wait
While waiting, trust.

In obedience, move;
knowing He will keep your feet from disaster.
In walking with Him, keep your heart clean
that you may hear Him when He speaks.

When the Spirit directs, *do*
When He chastises, *repent*
When He sends, *go*

23 Matthew 7:7.

Let Him sit on the throne of your heart
and let Him have the final say.
— 02/Jan/24.

69

Vigour

In the vigour of my youth, I will serve the Lord
and when I am old I will have no regrets.
For I used my bones well,
that He may be enthroned on my praises and
back-breaking dances.
That I may, while single, entertain only His Goodness and
promote His Business—
serving my Father, like an unmarried daughter.

Lord Jesus You have whispered 'wake up'
in my ears this morning and I have risen.
You have put light in my eyes that my first desire is You.
I have repented from my wanderings that You may lead me
aright;
I have rearranged my priorities in the order of You first.
In my youth, I will be bent to Your Will.
— 11/Sept/23.

70

Ihe nzuzo

Ihe nzuzo ufodu ka-ana eme ka
ha ba na nti ezi enyi
Ufodu ka-ana eme ka ha ba na nti
onye ihuru n'anya mgbe anaenweghi onye ozo ga-anu ya

Ufodu n'eso anyi ba na ana ini
Onweghi ihunanya ga-eme
ka amara ihe ibu n'obi nke inekwupataghi

Ma ka m juo gi,
onwere ihe iga ezonari
Onye mazuru ihe nine.

Secrets

Some you spill into the ears of a dear friend
Some you tell a lover after dark

And some you take to your grave
A kind of love cannot break that jar

But what can you hide from
the One who already knows all?
— 26/Apr/22.

71

That was You

It's this deep feeling that goes beyond words,
beyond quantification and anything physical

It's this void that only He can fill completely
It's this deep yearning for something more
Something reachable but so out of reach
Fully sated but never satisfied

It's peace, love, mercy and this deep knowledge
of being looked after, being cared for
being protected and provided for

It's Someone that listens and hears your heart
when your mouth has said so little
It's Someone that's intentional about you

Someone that aligns your every day so perfectly
that you barely notice it until you look back
and you realise with so wide a smile on your face
like a coconut split in two...

That was You. That was *God.*
— 13/Apr/21.

72

The wicked

The ones who choose wickedness,
        who do they call when
        their snares trap them?
The ones who do not believe,
        where do they go when walls
        rise up against them?

I call on God and He answers;
even when He does so with silence
it is better than the thousand voices
not of Him.

Abba lets me see Him.

If you trust in money,
        what happens when it flees?
If you trust in man
        what happens when he returns to dust?

I will trust in the One beyond this world

I will hope in the One above every other

How can a man have no allies beyond this world
when cruelty seeks to destroy him
as one created in the very image
of the Most High?
— 12/Jan/24.

73

I can't tell you

I can't tell you all I'm doing
I can't tell you where I'm heading
I can't tell you how it makes sense or not.

I can't tell you I have all the risks covered
That my plan is fail-proof
I can't even be certain that I know what I'm doing
I can't say that all the results you see were
intended results from smart calculations.

I CAN tell you though
        about the One who holds it all together.
I CAN tell you about the One
        who channels the wisdom of the ages
        through an ordinary conduit like me.

I CAN tell you about my fail-safe plan,
        the Man upstairs.
I CAN tell you about
        the sweetest Person I know.

See, I would be content if all
He would have me do
is worship at His Feet.
But He would hear none of that—
He convinced me that He's made me
for more, and I believe Him.

Who wouldn't, when He sings it
in such melodious tunes?
Again and again, each note softer
and more compassionate
like wine melting on the palette;
each sip multiplying the intoxication.

I have One who is my Father
Friend, Sponsor, Intercessor

I have One Who I am content with
beyond what the world could offer me.
Indeed, the Lord is my Shepherd; I have all I need.
— 17/Oct/22.

74

Second option

Sometimes, there is no one else to talk to
and that's when I remember You.
Sometimes loneliness arises within me
that I don't know if You can fill.

Do You get offended
that sometimes You're my second option?
That I know I should come here first
but instead, I tell all to a friend in one breath?

It's not because You're not listening,
I'm just impatient to hear You.
Yet a gaze from You
beats a thousand voices and whisperings.

I will wait for You.

You who understands my heart
my tears, my shrug and the
triple blink of my lids;

I will wait for You.
— 22/Dec/23.

75

Immune

How immune I feel when I'm with You;
I would slay a thousand foes.
How tender, my heart feels,
like it would burst from all that beating.

How quickly, my tongue rises to Your defence;
who would dare utter a bad word against You?
You're my heart
You're my life
What can separate our love?
— 13/Jan/24 (13/Apr/22).

76

Life's not simple

The simple is the complex, only well-hidden.
The simple is pain and suffering, behind a mask of
an understanding smile.
The simple is the unacknowledged and undermined
experiences that allow a snake to shed its skin and forget the pain of change.

The simple is the complex, diluted for the faint-hearted;
like pleasure is the harbinger of pain.
The simple is a clown, whose natural demeanour is a
mockery
to those who try to make sense of it
because it makes no sense.

The simple is *forgiveness and forgetfulness*
wrapped into a wreath and hung on the door at Christmas,
welcoming one and welcoming all.

The simple is an extended handshake after cutting words
and ears heavy laden with gossip.

The simple is a smile that never reaches the eyes
but will do until the crowd goes home.

The simple, is anything *but* life.
— 19/Oct/22.

77

Patient X

Give my mind sanity
Diagnose my insanity
Cure me of world-sickness
Purge me of emptiness

Hold my cold heart
Warm it with Your Love
When my heart goes silent
let me hear Your Voice

There's no hack to how He works
There's no totality of knowledge
Yesterday's method can be discarded
But if you stay, you'll see greater wonders.
— 28/Jan/24.

78

My desire

This is my desire
when I look out my window
watching life pass by;
hundreds of stories and dreams on two feet—

I wonder where I will stop telling my story
I wonder where others start to narrate it for me
I don't wonder for long—
Somehow, God has given me
a present mind;
fastened on the now
while He thinks of tomorrow.

To my heart, I say,
maybe all these plans
will not come to life.
Still my one desire
is to be where He wants me to be

in every moment
as long as He tarries.
— 09/Feb/24.

79

Wings

The Lord knows what He's doing
to make my life better.

Abba has stretched my mind to dream,
He says what things I want are not as far as they seem.
Abba has given me wings to fly,
He said only I can decide how high.

Abba has strengthened my hands to do,
a life of service will be my cue.
Abba has put grace in my strides,
there is peace, whether in high or low tides.
Abba has purged my soul of its fears;
I have also cast on Him, all of my cares.

Lead me, and I will follow;
direct me with Your eye, and I will go.
Not like the mule or horse
whose hearts have been made coarse.

As You carry me, I want to carry You along;
in every thought, action, and utterance of my tongue.
At the pace of grace, I move.
If You don't get the glory, I lose.
— 31/Dec/23.

80

The familiar

We often go back to the familiar:
faces, places, things,
solaces we're used to;
something about *the devil you know?*

Pain has no patience for change
New things would make it cringe
So we embrace thorn-filled arms
In here, we find our pseudo-calm
Soon, we'll be off again.
— 14/Apr/22.

81

Balm

Sometimes my mind goes numb
and my soul is weary...

But then my Jesus comes back,
His Words flow to my heart.
A healing balm that soothes.
Then I *remember*
and my healing occurs.
— 25/Dec/23.

82

Journey to You

At first, it is a bicycle
and we can barely carry ourselves.
This faith is fragile
and Your *Milk* nourishes our baby spirits.

Soon our bicycles can take on
the weight of one more,
and we ride together;
journeying towards You.

Then it's a car, a bigger vehicle;
we've formed a tribe
around Your Goodness.
Your Light binds us as glue.

Then we disperse;
for this journey is not about
how fast we can get to You
but how many we can bring with us.

We go, making disciples
who make disciples
because You are a gift
that keeps on giving.

Soon, it is not just a string of vehicles;
it is a long convoy
of people, who brought people
who brought people, that brought people
        to You.

Now we're on this narrow path;
gently treading
but boldly marching
to the gates of heaven.
— 09/Dec/21.

83

Savour

I'm learning to savour my fatigue.
Take pleasure in it…

I usually get things done
But on the days when I can't seem to move faster than a snail
I will learn to wallow in it
I will play slow songs to slow an already slow day

And to this end,
I will better appreciate the days
when my body does not fail me
or my mind acts like an overused knife.
— 08/Nov/22.

84

Njikota

Ana m ahu Jisos anya na anya
Mu na Jisos no na otu amara Chineke
Esom Mmuo nke Chineke na-aga ije
Emikpurum n'ime Mmuo nke Chineke

Abanyegom n'ime ihunanya Chineke
Dika mu na amaku Mmuo nke Chineke mgbe obuna
Nkpisi aka m ejidego onye nwem Jeso Kristi.

Ana m ahu Jisos anya na anya
Mu na Jisos no na otu amara Chineke
Esom Mmuo nke Chineke na-aga ije; Emikpurum
n'ime Mmuo nke Chineke

Abanyegom n'ime ihunanya Chineke
Dika mu na amaku Mmuo nke Chineke
mgbe obuna
Nkpisi aka m ejidego onye nwem
Jeso Kristi.

Linked

I've locked eyes with Jesus
I've fallen into a rhythm of grace
I've waded in the Holy Spirit

I'm hooked on God's love
As I lie in the Spirit's embrace
With my fingers linked in Christ's.

I've locked eyes with Jesus
I've fallen into a rhythm of grace
I've waded in the Holy Spirit

I'm hooked on God's love
as I lie in the Spirit's embrace
with my fingers linked in Christ's.

— 15/Oct/21.

85

The days when

For the days when you
don't want to be here;
don't want to turn your head
when you hear your name
and don't want to make sounds but be quiet.

Your thoughts rage
Your soul has gone quiet
Your eyes betray you
but no one is looking
and no one wants to know if you care
for the million things they say.

You want to go to the mountaintop, scream
Maybe pop a vein in the process
Anything to stop this numb feeling.

Pet your thoughts to quiet
Give your heart CPR[24]
Listen to the sound of silence

Stand unmoving in a shallow lake
Stare at the clouds and watch them change shape
Feel the wind in every orifice
Speak with every organ but your mouth

Don't just see these things
See the One behind them
Take heed not to exalt the created
over the Creator

Then drop yourself at His feet
Shed your pain

To be alive in Him
First, you must die.
— 13/Jan/24 (13/Apr/22).

24 Cardiopulmonary resuscitation (CPR) is a lifesaving technique that's useful in many emergencies in which someone's breathing or heartbeat has stopped.

86

Sonship

Entering into sonship,
I've never known a Father like this—
Super attentive to me,
Responding as I speak,
Holding my heart in His,
Whispering words of affection to me...

Loving me,
Showing me His Glory,
Directing me in His Wisdom,
Filling my heart with courage...

And all because
I tuned in to His Word;
daily examining myself in His Mirror
and making corrections.
I gave myself to worship

Life worship—
This living sacrifice
will never rise from the altar.
— 08/Jan/24.

87

Ibu aro

Onye nwem emewo ka idi mma ya
buru ibu aro nyem
Odighi ihe m ga-eme banyere ya
ma obughi igbasa ya

Onu m juputara n'ihe ogbugba ama
Obi m juputakwara karia

N'ihi nka, aga m agbasa ozi ahu
agaghim edebe ya n'onwem.

A burden

The Lord has made His Goodness
a burden to me
I have no choice but to share it…

My mouth is heavy with testimonies
My heart is full and overflows…

Oh! I have to share You
I cannot keep You to myself...
— 14/Jul/21.

88

Pain stop

One day
When He comes,
this ball of pain called the world will stop.
Go up in fire,
for the flood has already been here.

No more ups and downs
For The Master is stability.
The Good News is key to share—
Not money or things that die.

Can you find solutions
in a place that gave you problems?
So look above
Only Jesus saves.
— 04/Feb/24.

89

Broken silence

My head hurts
and soon, these tears will not be enough.
A broken silence takes over;
the tears keep dropping
but my heart does the crying…

For *more*
For *deeper*
For *His Glorification*
For *His Resplendence*
through me…

This yearning cannot be stopped;
I pray it only goes deeper
the more it is satisfied…

I want to see,

I want to hear,
I want to give everything I have;
Holy Spirit, take over.
— 28/Dec/21.

90

My first love

You loved me before I loved You.
You kept Your Eyes on me
even when my focus was everywhere but You.
And when You couldn't take the hurt anymore
You rescued me from myself.

Who am I that You are so mindful of me?
What have I ever done to deserve such love?
Nothing, absolutely nothing—
Yet, You deemed me worthy.

Oh Abba:
I will worship You with my life
with my lips, with everything I have.
I love You *deep*.
An eternity with You?
There's nothing else I'd rather do!
— 20/Sept/21.

91

Set my love

I have set my love upon You
I carry You in my heart
Give me strength to serve You
I want to
    put You in front
I want to
    go the extra mile for You
I want to

Jesus help me
I have nobody but You
Abba help me
Emi mimo, kaabo[25].
— 26/Dec/23.

25 'Holy Spirit, welcome' in Yoruba.

92

Untainted

This is what you do
if you suspect a brother has been
tainted by the world:

Do not be cruel,
is he not your kin?
Take his name to the Lord.

Ask the Father to
teach, correct and restore.
And if He sends you
let love be at your core.

If one part takes a hit,
is the whole body not in danger?
So get out your first aid kit,
let your knees hit the ground in prayer.

In each of us
Abba is pruning for purity.

So we count every loss
as pruning that shapes our identity.

The Lord hates mixture,
what is holy cannot be common.
His Body is set apart in nature;
no serving God and *mammon*[26].
— 12/Feb/24.

26 Matthew 6:24.

93

Drift

Lay down, breathe;
in, out, through your nose and teeth.
Hear your heartbeat against your skin
and for the noise within, let there be a famine.

Distil your thoughts to stillness;
in this silence you show yourself some kindness
Relax your muscle.
Stop the bustle, pause the hustle.

And let your eyelids close, don't peep
as you drift off to sleep.
— 14/Feb/24.

94

00:00

My heart is full
and pouring out
I don't want what You can give;
I want You.

I am not here out of duty
          or yet another request
I am here out of love;
          the one You first showed me.

I have gone through the day with You
but when I think that I have not sat attentively
to worship and sing my heart for You
my soul aches distinctly.

Now I am here,
I am limited by the words to
describe You, my deepest Lover.
Can I compare You with
the beauty of the things You have made?

You would wipe away the sea
like I would wipe a tear from my cheeks.
You would quench the sun
like I would quench a candle.

You would crumble the earth
like I would crumble a paper in my hands.
You would recall every living thing
with just a Word from Your lips.

You are perfect
My Lord, You are perfect
There is nothing out of place with You
Not a plan, not a will.

Taking pleasure in what You have made
Taking pleasure in me
Sitting with me and whispering sweet notes
of Your goodness into my ears
Like I am anything.

Your presence is the source
of my life and identity
It is with You I come alive
When I praise You, I know that I make You happy
and I want to do it even more.

What access to the King of the universe!
Your enormity amplifies my finite smallness

Still, all I want is to be where You would have me,
worshipping and loving You
Abba, take every glory due You.

May my needs not be
compared to Your will.
May Your Kingdom come first in my life
and in everything I have.

What do I need that is worth more than souls?
How can I not give to my King what He desires?
Jesus, purge me of everything not of You.

My beauty is that You love me
A King loves me
Now I am royalty
Clothed with His adoration
Bejewelled with His Name
Adorned with His prophecies

I inhale You and I exhale peace
and love and every good thing.
Oh be seated in my heart
Tighten Your hold over my soul.

How do I explain that You are closer than these hands?
I see You within me but not with these eyes
You hold me, I could never hold You
You fill my soul with the purest rhythms of life.

My heart is tight until I pour out Your worship
and spend myself at Your Feet
A stream's natural state is to flow, else contamination
My heart is Your stream of worship.

Lord, come closer;
make me Yours, completely.
Let me worship You until my dying day
Then wake me up to continue in eternity.
— 20/Feb/24.

95

Emesigo

Ebe m na-ahu ihe mgbochi
Chineke na-ahu olu ebube

Oburu na mu na Chineke ekpezigo,
enweghim otutu okwu n'ebe mmadu no.

It is settled

Where I see obstacles
God sees miracles

And if I settle it with God
I won't have to say much before men.
— 2022.

96

Searching

Seeking out my Lord
Searching for Him like a treasure
Searching for something more
What an intimate pleasure…

I am not looking for
something that can be found—
My Lord has no end.
This is not a trip that is round…

So this journey to Abba
has become my destination.
Fellowship with Him is my daily bread.
Upon His beauty is my constant meditation…

In Your presence
my identity unravels.
Looking at You,
I see who I really am…

There is a fellowship
          that sets me ablaze
There is a communion
          that lifts up my soul
There is a feasting
          that fills up my spirit

Satisfaction, intense completion
For I am a round hole
And Abba is a round peg
And this communion, is the fitting room.
— 27/Feb/24.

97

Funeral of dreams

My dreams in one hand
and a shovel in the other.
If you're wondering what,
you've happened upon a funeral.
            There is a cemetery nearby.

I've been carrying the weight
that I was commanded to lay down.
Did He not say His yoke is light?
Then this my burden has to go;
            be my audience as I lay it to rest.

Do not judge me yet;
I do not carry filth in these bags.
My Lord washed me clean long ago.
There is nothing here not of Him.
But let me tell you my mistake.

Why this funeral must happen is:
That I thought my will and His

could live side by side
That I thought I could do His thing
and do my thing as well.

You happened on this funeral,
but I did not happen upon this freedom.
My Lord directed me here in mercy.
For can I tell the One who has given me life
what to do with it?

The tears from my eyes
have washed away my ambition;
every dream and goal is dead—
six feet under.
The cold earth nods as I give it one last pat.

Let my only dreams be those
He has given me.
No more ambitions, no goals
just what He wants.
Let my life be marked by
things I could never have imagined
because I gave it to Him.

I pick up obedience and availability and hunger
but I also carry the shovel home—
perhaps I'll see something else
that needs to be buried.
— 29/Feb/24.

98

Ihunanya[27]

I see you in my eyes
I see you

Not the labels
the world has put on you
I see you
Not the flaws you note
when you gaze at your reflection
I see you

I see the kindness in your eyes
and the nervous giggle when you're surprised.
I see your passion for the things you love
and your tenderness for the truth.
I see your strength in all of these...

27 This is how the Igbos describe 'love'. It loosely translates to 'I see you in my eyes - the object of my affection and attention'.

This is not the kind of love you need to show off
This is not the kind of love displayed on the altar of human validation
This love needs no input from the world

This is the kind you give to the Most High to shield
This is the kind you nurture
and pour yourself into
bit by bit, piece by piece, flaw by flaw.

This is the kind of love that swallows you whole,
sheltering your intricacies.
And the world sees you happy,
but they have no clue.
— 02/Mar/24.

99

Imela[28]

Thank You
For the grin that reaches my eyes
  and the smirk that graces one cheek.
For the days when I am not wise
  and the days my flesh seems at its peak.

Thank You
For music I can dance to
  and the ones I wipe my tears to.
For the silence that reveals You
  and Your Commands that make me do.

Thank You
For an embrace of compassion and wisdom
For many a laughter and many sorrows
through loved ones; some planned, some random—
People with whom I'll see many tomorrows.

---

28 Igbo word for 'thank you'.

Thank You
For butterflies in my belly, living and dead
        and the strengthening of my heart.
For the faith to look ahead
        and when I fall, head back to the start.

Thank You
For a dream beyond this world
        and a hope of an eternity with You.
And for a chance to cry '*Holy*!'
'*Holy are You Lord!*'[29]
— 02/Mar/24.

29 Revelation 4:8-11.

100

Soft life

To the one who desires a soft life,

Lend me an ear, please,
And I will tell you what a soft life means:

It is not merrymaking that
excessively indulges in worldly pleasures.
It is not laziness that wants to
eat what it did not work for, no endeavours.

It is not lasciviousness and a mind
that claims '*my body, my choice*[30]'.
It is not leeway to act on every thought that
comes to mind, from the devil's voice.
It is not financial freedom and getting what you want, when you want it,

30 Popular phrase used to indicate the need for personal choice on personal being without external influence or aid often used in protest of conventional or conservative views on modern deviations of character or life choices.

even self-will destroys.

It is an elastic heart that expands to abase and abound.
It is a mind that thinks often and takes pleasure in doing so;
so its mouth utters only blessings all around.

It is a meek and lowly heart, on which
God has written His law of love.
It is a head bowed at the Throne of Mercy,
willing to go even before He sends—Yahweh, above.

A soft life is the Christ Life...
— 07/Feb/24.

A note to you, my friend

I am discovering that poetry helps me tell a story in the shortest form possible. It removes the unnecessary parts and highlights only the core because there is not so much space. So, a story is broken into pieces and told.

Unlike a story, a poem does not focus so much on the narrative that the message is easy to neglect. Rather, the narrative is present but muted while the message is emphasized. This also helps me see outside myself.

In all of these poems, I am telling stories my eyes have seen, albeit with a diluted narrative and overemphasised message. Many of these stories are ongoing, since I am living them, so a feeling of incompleteness may arise after reading some of them. I will admit, however, that the suspense is partially intentional. I do love open stories, to let the reader's mind wander even more.

Regardless, the Message is Christ. If, for some reason, you do not know Him as intimately as you know you should, I give you this Message of reconciliation. Jesus wants you and now, tomorrow is too far. Read and confess **Romans 10:9** -

> **That if thou shalt confess with thy mouth the Lord Jesus, and shalt believe in thine heart that God hath raised him from the dead, thou shalt be saved.**

then send an email to **maranathammxxi@gmail.com** if you would like some help on your new journey.

I hope you have enjoyed reading these poems as much as I loved writing them. More than anything, I hope Christ has softened your heart and you let Him continue to. I would love to hear from you too, questions, contributions, testimonies–everything! You can connect with me by scanning the QR code below:

Visitmaranatha.com

Come back here whenever your heart desires softness,
See you, shortly,
Maranatha, The Softie.

Other Works

The Devotional Cheat Code: A practical step-by-step on how to stay consistent in your devotion to God - A book with practical and easily applicable 'cheats' for anyone struggling with consistency in their devotion to and fellowship with God.

All you have to be is Light - This book gets rid of common Christian stereotypes. It connects personal/character development to the spread of the Gospel, highlighting the importance of evangelism for all Christians.

You can get these books at - **visitmaranatha.com/shop**

About the Author

Maranatha (Favour Nnaemeka) is an Evangelist whose yielding to God's call upon her life has blessed many people. From writing soul-piercing pieces to convert the souls of people to Christ to stewarding an intercessory Christian community called Jars of Clay, Maranatha is dedicated to her Father's Work—'Who wants all people to be saved and come to the knowledge of the truth'.

She also runs a blog on Visitmaranatha.com, where she shares personal experiences in her Walk of Faith as well as resources to help Christians grow in their faith.

She is the author of *The Devotional Cheat Code,* a Christian guide to maintaining consistency in our walk with God, and *All you have to be is Light,* a book that connects personal and character development to the spread of the Gospel through evangelism.

This is her third published book.

Manufactured by Amazon.ca
Acheson, AB

30468672R00139